Age of Bees
© Tira Palmquist
Trade Edition, 2015
ISBN 978-1-63092-070-8

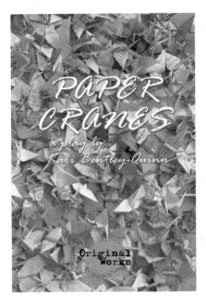

Paper Cranes by Kari Bentley-Quinn

Synopsis: PAPER CRANES is the story of Mona, a recent widow obsessed with the Japanese ritual of folding origami cranes as she grieves the loss of her beloved husband. Mona's teenage daughter, Maddie, is struggling with the demands of her bereft mother and her sexual identity, and begins a romantic relationship with an older woman named Julie. Meanwhile, Julie's best friend, Amy, has begun an intense S&M relationship with a man who is guarding a dark secret. From there, the stories of these five people intertwine, revealing the lasting scars of grief and the desire to be loved.

Cast Size: 1 Male, 4 Females

AGE OF BEES
by
TIRA PALMQUIST

*To [name],
who saved the
Bees!*

SYNOPSIS

The bees have gone, and the world struggles to keep up with the resulting ecological and economic changes. In the midst of this, we meet Mel, a young woman who has found sanctuary on an agricultural compound, where there's food and safety. She works alongside other girls, also orphans or castoffs. Sarah and Zed, who run the farm, hope that their next child will be a boy; Sarah is at the end of her fertility, however, and, to her dismay, Mel stands next in line to carry children for Zed. Into this uncertain sanctuary steps Jonathan, an independent field researcher who collects samples of plants to forestall additional ecological devastation. Meeting Mel provides a glimmer of other kinds of scientific riches on this compound, and he is determined to take her with him. Zed's history of violence makes any escape a dangerous proposition. Still, there's the hope that something new can grow, that something good can come from the ruined world they struggle to make theirs.

ACKNOWLEDGMENTS

The World Premiere of AGE OF BEES was produced in 2012 by MadLab Theater (Artistic Director, Andy Batt) in Columbus, OH. The production was directed by Jim Azelvandre, assisted by Aran Carr, with the following cast and crew:

Mel	Mary Beth Griffith
Jonathan	Travis Horseman
Deborah	Lexy Weixel
Sarah	Courtney Deuser

The Midwest Premiere of AGE OF BEES was produced in 2015 by Tesseract Theater (Artistic Director, Taylor Gruenloh) in St. Louis, MO. The production was directed by Daniel J. Betzler, assisted by Michelle Henley, with the following cast and crew:

Mel	Mikayla Sherfy
Jonathan	Andrew Rea
Deborah	Katie Palazzola
Sarah	Tonya Darabcsek

CAST BREAKDOWN:

DEBORAH   Late teens.
MEL   22, but looks younger.
SARAH   Late 30s.
JONATHAN   Late 20s.

The playwright strongly encourages casting from any ethnicity for all of the roles.

TIME
In the future.

SETTING
Unit set should incorporate at least three different playing areas. First, a defunct orchard, with a few very old apple trees: the trunks are gnarled, twisted, some bending toward the earth as if under a heavy burden. There are also a few models of what used to be essential farm machinery, in various states of disrepair or disarticulation.

Another playing area functions as the house -- usually a bedroom or sitting room of a simple, older style farm house.

Then other playing areas can be suggested with a few lights. All the action should move seamlessly from scene to scene with no set change.

Special thanks

The passages read on Page 59 are from *The ABC and XYZ of Bee Culture*, by A. I. Root, published by the A. I. Root Company, 1962.

AGE OF BEES has received a reading at Theatricum Botanticum (Topanga Canyon, CA) in the summer of 2008. The play was the winner of Company of Angels' New Play Festival, "Visions of Dystopia." Company of Angels then produced a workshop production of the play in June 2009. In June 2011, 9Thirty Theatre presented a reading of AGE OF BEES as part of their SEEDS Development Series.

AGE OF BEES

ACT ONE

(In the darkness: we hear snatches of very fuzzy radio stations, and the whine and static of switching up and down the dial. Some stations seem very far away, some playing what seems to be music from another century, others seeming to be carrying on oddly unprofessional conversations about the state of roads or the price of goods. Only some of the reports are from actual news organizations -- some are clearly broadcasts from someone's basement or compound.)

RADIO TRANSMISSION: We got reports of the Cardinal Switchgrass Toxic Cleanup field burning now ...and the fumes are pretty bad there, so you better give a big berth... uh, winds out of the west, ten to twenty miles per hour -- *(Static.)* ...official count has reached 47,000 but unofficial reports put it much higher. Rumors of mass graves -- *(Static.)* ...until the infection rates decrease, the governor has shut down traffic on all routes -- *(Static.)* ...And now we're getting reports about shortages of fresh produce, everywhere -- *(Static.)* ...resistance to gentamicin, vancomycin, ciproflaxicin, and the failure of the new 2nd generation drugs have led to new attempts with bacteriophages -- *(Static.)* ...the Cuyahoga camp is full. Please note: the Cuyahoga camp is full -- *(Static.)* ...the joint expedition to find colonies of apis mellifera has been called off due to widespread threat of disease. It's unknown when another expedition -- *(Static.)*

(Early morning light on a very old orchard. Half the trees are dead, the other half are dying and, even though it's mid-May, they're not in blossom. In the branches of one

8

tree, is a girl of 16 swings, trying to tune into some music on a small radio. This is DEBORAH. She's dressed in a simple skirt and t-shirt -- the skirt tucked between her legs -- the pieces from different decades, oddly put together.)

RADIO TRANSMISSION: ...No, those masks are no good. The cartridges give out too quick, and then you're breathing in all sorts of crap ...

(O.S., there's the crackle of a walkie talkie, and DEB-ORAH, surprised, drops her radio. She slips down from the tree, quickly turns off the radio, and listens.)

MEL (O.S.): Yes, I'm checking on them -- Yes...

WALKIE TALKIE: *(Mumbling, unintelligible.)*

(DEBORAH quickly runs to some old machinery, slides the radio into a hiding place, and scrambles back up the tree, to hide herself in the leaves.)

MEL (O.S.): What? No. The perimeter sensors. Unit 10. Probably just a loose wire.

(A young person enters, dressed in work pants, heavy boots, a sturdy shirt and vest, adjusting something on her walkie talkie. This is MEL. She's about 22, though looks like she could be much younger. From the way she's dressed and her close-cropped hair, one would have a hard time guessing her sex.)

MEL (CONT'D): *(Into the walkie talkie.)* I'll check the rest, too, while I'm at it. *(Static.)* What? *(Then a female voice cuts in.)* Sarah? *(Under her breath.)* Shit. *(Into the walkie talkie.)* Hold on, Sarah. I'm in the old or-chard. Just... wait 'til I get back up to the house.

(She slips the walkie talkie into a loop on her workbelt, which also holds a number of useful tools. She carries a mid-sized pack on her back, and she slips that off.)

(MEL looks around, and then goes to the old machines, and opens up a metal panel. She pulls out what appears to be an old pesticide jug. The top section has been cut to function as a lid, which she pulls off, to reveal a clever place to store her valuables. She pulls out a sheaf of papers, magazines, other remnants of printed material from the container. She takes out what appears to be a few tattered sections of a newspaper from a pocket, carefully puts them with the rest of her collection, and places the sheaf back into the pesticide container.)

(DEBORAH remains unnoticed, but is tense, alert.)

(Lid shoved back on top, MEL returns the container to its hiding place next to several other containers. She walks to the edge of the orchard, and stops at what looks like a tall metal fence post, with a small solar array and a sensor unit at the top of it. She begins to climb the little footholds in the pole until she gets up near the panel. She slings her leg around the pole to hold herself in place and free up her hands to work. The walkie talkie squeals, but she does not answer it.)

MEL (CONT'D): Just hang on. I can't be everywhere at once.

(Using her knife, she pries open a metal panel just below the solar array, and examines the wiring there. Meanwhile, the voice on the walkie talkie continues.)

WALKIE TALKIE: *(Female voice.)* We were in the late blooms, and she just disappeared. None of the girls saw her leave *(Static)* she just *(Static)* she was there, and then --

(MEL continues to work on the repairs while she mumbles to herself, ignoring the walkie talkie.)

MEL: God...

WALKIE TALKIE: Mel! Mel, pick up.

MEL: *(Still ignoring the walkie talkie.)* Calm down, Sarah.

WALKIE TALKIE: She's gone. Deborah's run off --

MEL: *(Still ignoring the walkie talkie.)* She'll come back.

WALKIE TALKIE: Mel, she's gone! I was just in the *(Static.)* --

MEL: *(Finally picking up the walkie talkie.)* Look, Sarah, I'm in the middle of something here!

WALKIE TALKIE: She's not in the house or her bedroom... Oh Lord...

(From a distance, the voice of the walkie talkie comes closer, and then, a woman of about 39 or 40 enters, talking into the walkie talkie as she does. This is SARAH. She is about 5 months pregnant, but walks with some effort. She's dressed in more feminine clothes than MEL. Still, she wears workboots.)

SARAH: *(Still talking into the walkie talkie.)* I've checked the house, out by the Empires, the Northern Spy -- nothing.

(DEBORAH clings to the tree.)

11

MEL: (*In response to Sarah's arrival.*) What the hell...?

SARAH: (*Sees Mel.*) Oh! Mel! Have you seen Deborah?

(*SARAH turns off her walkie talkie, and puts it in her bag.*)

MEL: What are you doing out here?

SARAH: Deborah's gone.

MEL: She's probably taking a nap somewhere.

SARAH: She could be hurt!

MEL: I doubt that.

SARAH: She could wander too far, and then -- (*A cramp in her side.*) Oh!

MEL: Sarah...?

SARAH: It's nothing. Just a hitch.

MEL: You need to sit down.

SARAH: (*The cramping becomes more intense.*) Lord!

MEL: Sit down!

(*SARAH lowers herself onto a stump, or rock, or over-turned barrow.*)

(*MEL uncaps a small metal canteen and hands it to SARAH, who takes a long drink.*)

SARAH: (*Looking around.*) Where on earth are we?

MEL: The old orchard.

SARAH: Goodness. I really did get turned around. What are you doing here?

MEL: Sensors. Mice are eating the wiring again, or something.

SARAH: Oh. (*Regarding the trees.*) Oh, yes. Crimson King.

MEL: What?

SARAH: I think that's what my grandfather said these were. Crimson King -- or Chesney? Beautiful apples, they were. (*Sighs.*) Poor things. There's just no use for them anymore, is there. Zed says they'd make nice furniture. Or firewood.

MEL: You'd cut 'em down?

SARAH: Oh, no! This was Grandpa Charles' original stand, and they'll stay until the Lord takes them down.

MEL: What about the rest?

SARAH: What about 'em?

MEL: I mean, these are dead -- And the rest aren't too far behind them.

SARAH: These are just old, that's all. Our trees are fine. They're fine.

(SARAH takes another long drink, sighs.)

MEL: You shouldn't be running around like this.

SARAH: *(Sighs deeply.)* Four months left.

MEL: It'll go quickly.

SARAH: I don't mean to complain. This one feels heavier somehow.

MEL: A big boy, then.

SARAH: *(She smiles, despite herself.)* We'll see...

MEL: *(Beat.)* Now come on -- let's get you out of the heat.

SARAH: Oh, fine.

(SARAH hands the canteen back to MEL, who goes to replace it in her pack. At that moment, MEL catches a glimpse of DEBORAH in the tree, but says nothing.)

MEL: You should head back up. It's a long walk.

SARAH: I'll be fine.

MEL: You're a big fatty, and you need your nap.

SARAH: Look for Deborah for me?

MEL: Don't worry. She'll turn up. *(Quick glance up at the tree.)* Now go.

SARAH: Wait. (*Closes her eyes, and holds her hands out in prayer.*) Lord, I come to you your humble servant. (*It's clear from MEL's response that she takes none of this seriously.*) Dear Lord, hear me. I ask you for the quick and safe return of Deborah to us now that you have blessed her with tongues of fire. May we never doubt your love, and may Deborah find serenity in the heavy mantle you've given to her. And be with Mel, to help her know your truth and light. Amen.

(*SARAH looks to MEL, expectantly.*)

MEL: Oh. (*Beat.*) Amen.

SARAH: Now. (*Holding out her hands to MEL.*) Help me up.

MEL: This is why you shouldn't be two feet from a rocking chair. (*Getting SARAH on her feet.*) You shouldn't worry about Deborah. She's not as delicate as you think.

SARAH: She's been touched by the spirit. (*As she exits.*) She's a child of God, Mel -- a child of God...

(*And she's gone. MEL walks over to the tree, and looks up into the branches.*)

MEL: Child of god my ass.

DEBORAH: Hey!

MEL: Get down. Now.

DEBORAH: You're a bitch, Mel.

MEL: Oh! Should I call her back?

DEBORAH: God! No!

MEL: So where were you going this time?

DEBORAH: Nowhere.

MEL: Ever since you ran away --

DEBORAH: I didn't run away.

MEL: Only because you got caught.

DEBORAH: (*Laughs.*) But I was filled with the Holy Spirit, Mel...

MEL: And now your mother watches your every move.

DEBORAH: Oh, she does not. She fell asleep while we were in the Pippins.

MEL: And you didn't think she'd notice when she woke up? Or that the other girls wouldn't care?

DEBORAH: The other girls like me.

MEL: That doesn't mean they'll keep doing your work. We have to get through the late blooms before the fall -- we have rows and rows to finish, and it's getting late in the season.

DEBORAH: You worry too much.

MEL: Let's call her back, huh?

(MEL takes her walkie talkie out of its holster.)

(Suddenly, DEBORAH gasps, and her eyes roll back in her head, her body contorted in some vaguely cruciform shape. As she twitches and writhes, she speaks in a guttural gibberish, which increases in pitch and volume until she cries out and falls to the ground. After a beat, she begins to laugh.)

DEBORAH: *(Looking up at MEL.)* You have to admit: that's pretty good.

MEL: You don't worry I'll tell her?

DEBORAH: She wouldn't believe you. I'm the child of God, Mel. You're the heathen.

MEL: That's not funny.

DEBORAH: Come on, Mel --

MEL: What are you doing way out here, anyway?

DEBORAH: I just wanted to be alone.

MEL: You've got hiding places.

DEBORAH: So?

MEL: *(More suspicious.)* What were you doing out here?

DEBORAH: Nothing! Never mind! I'm going!

MEL: Oh, no you're not. I'm walking you back. Just hold on a minute.

DEBORAH: Come on. Just say you saw me asleep in the garden.

MEL: Now you want me to lie for you, too?

DEBORAH: Mel!

MEL: No. Now sit, and wait for me to finish. Sit!

(DEBORAH sits, reluctantly obedient, as MEL returns to her repairs.)

DEBORAH: Jeez. Fine. *(Pause as she watches MEL work.)* I wasn't running away.

MEL: If you say so.

DEBORAH: That other time or now. I wasn't.

MEL: You go pretty far for not running away.

DEBORAH: I just get sick of them. Don't you?

MEL: No.

DEBORAH: Well, you don't have to spend all day with them.

MEL: I spend plenty of time with them.

DEBORAH: I guess. It's just... you're different. *(Beat.)* I'm in the middle. Too old to be a kid, not old enough to be taken seriously. *(Beat.)* Do you think I'm pretty?

MEL: What?

DEBORAH: Am I pretty? As pretty as my mother?

MEL: Sure you are.

DEBORAH: (*Beat.*) All I wanted was a few minutes alone. That's all.

MEL: Well, in the future, take your minutes somewhere else.

DEBORAH: Mel --

MEL: I'm not gonna tell you again: The old equipment is rusty and full of nasty things. Plus, it's too close to the perimeter.

DEBORAH: You're out here all the time.

MEL: To look after the sensors.

DEBORAH: Uh huh.

MEL: And it's not all the time.

DEBORAH: Really?

MEL: You have your hiding places, and I have mine. I'm not gonna tell you again: Stay out.

DEBORAH: Or what?

MEL: I know you don't believe me, but there are real dangers out there, Deborah. If you'd gotten far enough, you would have seen. And there are worse dangers you can't see --

DEBORAH: Oh, yeah. I know. Loads of dangers. I know.

MEL: You do.

DEBORAH: (*As if reciting some frequently repeated admonition.*) The old orchard is too close to the stream, which leads to the road, which carries travelers, who carry diseases --

MEL: All of which is true.

DEBORAH: OK. OK. I know.

MEL: Then act like it. (*Beat.*) You need to stay put or run off like you mean it.

DEBORAH: I'm not running off -- (*Beat.*) Fine.

MEL: Good.

DEBORAH: Well, you should be careful too. (*Pointing to the Mel's hiding place.*) I know what you've got there.

MEL: Oh. So?

DEBORAH: Zed wouldn't like it.

MEL: And you're going to tell him? Tricky, that: to tell him what you saw, without saying that you were there to see it. You know what your father's like.

DEBORAH: Step-father.

MEL: Whatever.

(*Brief pause. Deborah smiles at her.*)

DEBORAH: So, if you can keep my secret...

MEL: Deborah...

DEBORAH: I can keep yours. (*Beat.*) Deal?

MEL: Fine. Now, I need some tape for that wiring. There's no way I'm gonna fix this alarm without it. (*Hopping down from the sensor unit.*) Come on. I'll walk you back.

DEBORAH: Mel, come on. Just a couple more minutes...

MEL: Sarah told me to find you.

DEBORAH: And you always do what you're told?

MEL: Let's go.

(*They exit. OS, we hear the voices of several young girls, talking, laughing, singing. Afternoon shadows lengthen.*)

(*Then, a man enters the grove, dressed in plain, sturdy clothes. He carries a large pack, perhaps with a makeshift crutch; he's hopping on one foot, clearly in pain.*)

JONATHAN: Ow, ow, ow... (*Pausing to get his balance.*) Oh, shit.

(*He takes off his pack and leans it against the tree, then tries to put weight on his ankle again. He winces.*)

JONATHAN (CONT'D): God damn it. (*He sits on the stump or rock or barrow, and begins taking off his boot and sock.*) It's swelling. Damn it.

(He fishes through the pack, and takes out an old military field telephone. Cranks it several times. Listens for the response on the other end.)

JONATHAN (CONT'D): Who's this? Hey -- Andrew. It's Jonathan. (*Pause.*) Jonathan. I know I was supposed to be back. I got a problem here -- (*Pause.*) Let me talk to Thomas, OK? (*Pause, massages his ankle.*) Hey, Tom. (*Pause.*) Well, the thing is... I twisted my fuckin' ankle. (*Pause.*) Don't tell me that. I know that. (*Pause.*) Yes, well, I won't be getting any farther tonight. (*Pause.*) Fine. (*Pause.*) Fine. (*Looking around.*) I don't know if I'm in the right place though. I mean, there are trees, but if someone told you they were productive... Man. There's nothing here. Not from where I'm sitting anyway. (*Pause.*) Yeah. Fine. I'll camp out here, and check the place out in the morning. Though I don't know if I can start my bike like this. (*Pause.*) Don't send Andrew. Andrew's a pussy. (*Pause.*) Yes, I'll check in. OK? OK.

(He hangs up the phone, returns it to his pack. He tries to find a comfortable position.)

JONATHAN (CONT'D): God. Damn. It.

(Finally comfortable, he begins to doze. In the distance, we hear the voices of the young girls, joining in some work song.)

(Afternoon shadows lengthen.)

(Then, MEL jogs into the orchard to return to the busted sensor. She sees JONATHAN, and stops abruptly.)

(She takes out her knife, and slowly approaches him.)

(MEL picks up a large stick or metal pole and prods his injured foot.)

MEL: Hey, you!

(The pain jolts through him -- and he gives a loud yelp of pain.)

MEL (CONT'D): Shut up!

JONATHAN: What the hell --

MEL: Don't move --

JONATHAN: Jesus!

MEL: *(Brandishing her weapon.)* Stay right there!

JONATHAN: OK! But don't hit me. Again.

MEL: I just poked you.

JONATHAN: Well, it hurt.

MEL: How'd you get here?

JONATHAN: How'd you get here?

MEL: Stop it! How'd you get in? *(Looking up at the sensors.)* Shit...

JONATHAN: I was crossing that creek and I slipped --

(JONATHAN starts to show her his ankle.)

MEL: Just stay put! Stop!

JONATHAN: Take it easy, take it easy. (*Referring to her knife.*) And maybe you want to put that away, son.

(*A brief pause.*)

MEL: You'd better get out of here.

JONATHAN: First, you tell me to stay put, now you tell me --

MEL: Hey! Just get up -- slowly -- and get the hell out of here.

JONATHAN: Look. I've had an accident. (*Showing her his ankle.*) See that?

MEL: I don't give a rat's ass.

JONATHAN: (*Overdramatizing the injury.*) It might be broken.

MEL: It's not. (*Beat.*) Come on! Get up!

JONATHAN: Or what. You'll beat me senseless?

MEL: Don't think I won't!

JONATHAN: Do I look dangerous to you?

MEL: I'm telling you, for the last goddamned time --

JONATHAN: Come on! I'm injured! Hungry! Completely defenseless! (*She backs off a bit. He reaches down to rub his ankle.*) You really got me good, kid.

MEL: (*Referring to his ankle.*) It's just sprained.

JONATHAN: So?

MEL: So: If you bound it up --

JONATHAN: What.

MEL: (*Beat.*) Then you could go.

JONATHAN: OK. Jesus. (*Looking in his pack.*) I don't think I have anything though.

MEL: I might. I mean, if it will get you to leave.

JONATHAN: Gee, I don't know. The hospitality here is so warm, and friendly.

(*Keeping her knife close, she starts to take a few things out of her pack.*)

MEL: (*Producing some grafting tape.*) We can try this.

JONATHAN: Tape?

MEL: Grafting tape. It works for broken branches. (*Shrugs.*) Come on.

JONATHAN: Yes, sir.

(*He hikes up his trouser leg to expose the injured ankle.*)

MEL: Put it up on your pack or something.

(*He does so, and she begins bandaging his ankle, working quietly, firmly.*)

JONATHAN: (*Lying.*) I guess I'm kinda lost. (*She doesn't respond.*) Is this... some kind of farm or something? (*Again, she doesn't respond.*) Hey! Ow! Take it easy, will you?

MEL: Sorry.

JONATHAN: It's OK. (*Beat.*) I'm Jonathan. (*No response.*) And you are...?

MEL: What?

JONATHAN: Your name. What's your name.

MEL: Why?

JONATHAN: Just trying to be friendly.

MEL: Oh. Mel.

JONATHAN: Mel. Hi, Mel. I'm Jonathan.

MEL: You said that.

JONATHAN: I did.

MEL: Not that I give a damn.

JONATHAN: Jesus, you have some mouth on you.

MEL: (*Lying.*) Sorry.

JONATHAN: You live here, Mel?

MEL: You ask a lot of questions.

JONATHAN: I'm a curious guy.

MEL: You shouldn't be.

JONATHAN: I think you have to ask questions.

MEL: No, you don't.

JONATHAN: How else do you find out about things?

MEL: Maybe you don't need to know. (*Beat.*) There. You're done.

(She grabs her knife again, and stands at a distance, as he replaces his boot.)

JONATHAN: I told you. I'm not dangerous.

MEL: That's what you say.

JONATHAN: I give you my word.

MEL: Zed would say that makes you one cheap bastard.

JONATHAN: Zed?

MEL: Zedekiah.

JONATHAN: Are you making that up?

MEL: No.

JONATHAN: Poor Zed.

MEL: What?

JONATHAN: It's a sad name. A sad name and a sad place. Look at these old things...

MEL: Well, these trees don't produce. But -- (*Shuts up.*)

JONATHAN: But what?

MEL: Nothing.

JONATHAN: You've got others? (*Silence.*) You must. I mean, I can smell the blossoms.

MEL: There's no way you can smell that from here.

JONATHAN: Ah ha!

MEL: Shit.

JONATHAN: What kinds of trees? Can I see them?

MEL: No. (*Beat.*) Stand and see how it does.

(JONATHAN hoists himself up, steadying himself with the tree.)

JONATHAN: The tape feels good.

MEL: Well? Come on. Put weight on it.

JONATHAN: Jesus, you're bossy. OK. Here goes.

(JONATHAN gingerly steps down on the injured ankle, gradually putting more weight on it, until -- he yelps, and stumbles back to the ground.)

JONATHAN (CONT'D): Sorry. (*Sitting back down.*) Nice try.

MEL: What are you doing?

JONATHAN: I'm not going anywhere tonight.

MEL: But --

JONATHAN: Look: You can either put me out of my misery or let me camp out here until I can walk.

MEL: You don't understand --

JONATHAN: How about -- one night. To start. If I make any trouble, you can drive me off. (*Beat.*) Just one problem: I'm running low on supplies --

(*He heaves his pack closer, and MEL looks toward the house, nervously. He takes out several things out of his pack, including some papers, a bundle of pencils held together with a rubber band, and a number of small tools.*)

JONATHAN (CONT'D): If you could spare any food --

MEL: Forget it.

JONATHAN: I mean, for a trade. Come on...

(*Then, a few books emerge from the pack, which catches MEL's attention.*)

MEL: Wait. (*Eyeing the books.*) A trade?

JONATHAN: Yeah. What do you need ... (*Starts to lay out a few small tools that might be of interest.*) Harmonica? Compass? Flint? Take your pick.

MEL: (*Points to the books.*) What about those?

JONATHAN: Oh... Sure.

MEL: Any of them?

JONATHAN: (*Picking through them.*) Well, not this one. Or this one. And... I need this one.

MEL: (*Quickly grabbing the one book left.*) So this one then.

JONATHAN: (*Begrudgingly.*) Fine.

MEL: (*Reading the cover.*) "The ABC and XYZ of Bee Culture." Must be old.

JONATHAN: Ancient. Deal?

(He holds out his hand to shake on it, but MEL just stands up, leaving the book on the ground.)

MEL: OK. I'll be back.

JONATHAN: Aren't you going to take it?

MEL: Doesn't seem fair to take it before you have your trade. (*Beat.*) Now -- You need to stay put.

JONATHAN: Yes sir.

MEL: I'm serious. You can't wander anywhere -- You need to stay right here.

JONATHAN: I'm not going anywhere. Believe me. But you're coming back, right?

MEL: Yeah.

JONATHAN: Promise?

MEL: No. But I'll be back.

(She exits.)

JONATHAN: OK, then, Mel.

(He takes a small handcrank radio and maps out of his back, cranks it several times, and begins to dial in to a favorite station.)

RADIO TRANSMISSION: …all the way up to the Finger Lakes. Just be careful is all -- *(Changes channel.)* …we've got reports of new infection zones posted by the governor, so mark these counties: Erie, Lorraine, Medina, Wayne -- *(Changes channel.)* No signs of Viola purpurea, pedunculata SPP at 46.78101 N, 92.11797 W…

(Happy, he turns to the maps.)

RADIO TRANSMISSION: …Vaccinium occidentale no longer at 44.96185 N, 93.26684 W -- and, um -- a single specimen of Celtis douglasii, pallida at 47.33341 N, 93.37179 W…

(He begins to mark locations as the crackling voice continues to list plants and the latitude and longitude where they no longer exist.)

(As afternoon gives way to evening, crickets begin to call out in the growing dusk.)

(Finally, MEL returns, a bag bulging with various items. She stops at some distance, watching JONATHAN as he

pores over his maps. Just then, the angry male voice erupts from her walkie talkie, and JONATHAN quickly turns.)

WALKIE TALKIE: (*Male voice grumbling.*) Sarah. Goddamn it, Sarah...

(MEL turns down the sound.)

JONATHAN: Shit. You scared me.

MEL: Sorry. What's all that?

JONATHAN: Work.

MEL: I didn't mean to interrupt.

JONATHAN: It's OK.

(He puts aside the maps. She hands over a small parcel with bread, hardboiled eggs, a tomato. Her knife remains in her other hand.)

MEL: Here.

JONATHAN: Thanks.

MEL: Sorry that's all.

JONATHAN: It's fine. (*Unpacking it.*) Better than fine.

(He finds the tomato, which he eats. She walks toward the map, curious.)

MEL: OK. Good. I'll -- try to check in before daylight.

(The male voice on the walkie talkie grumbles again, and she steps away from him.)

JONATHAN: You're going?

(She nods.)

JONATHAN (CONT'D): You're not going to have any?

(She shakes her head.)

JONATHAN (CONT'D): Suit yourself.

(He unwraps a few eggs from a cloth, and she lets her knife hang loosely at her side.)

JONATHAN (CONT'D): Hard boiled?

MEL: Yes.

JONATHAN: *(He cracks one on his head, and begins peeling it.)* Nice. The last eggs I ate were raw. A pigeon, I think. *(She smiles, finding herself interested in his story.)* It's not very nice to eat raw eggs, but when I'm out, I've learned to eat what I can, when I can. And raw eggs aren't as bad as other things I could have eaten. Well, I'd never eat a rat or anything. I'm not stupid. *(Eating the first egg. A moan of pleasure.)* Oh my god...

MEL: *(Beat.)* Who are you?

JONATHAN: Excuse me?

MEL: I've heard about men like you.

JONATHAN: Men like me? I'm not sure what that means.

MEL: People who wander about, seeming to look for a handout, but they're there to strip the copper wiring from your house, or something like that.

JONATHAN: Well, I'm not here to do anything like that.

MEL: Then what are you doing?

JONATHAN: Currently, I am a hobbled eater of eggs.

MEL: A thief?

JONATHAN: I'm not stealing anything.

MEL: You have my food.

JONATHAN: We made a trade.

MEL: Oh... Right.

JONATHAN: So I'm not a thief.

MEL: A drifter then. Well, that's what Zed calls them. He says you don't think of them as robbers. They steal right in front of you, smiling as if they belong there. A robber you might chase out of your house. A drifter, well, you might just hand them your money before they've asked where it's hidden.

JONATHAN: I'd bet you Zed's never seen any kind of robber. Or drifter. Outside of his own imagination, that is. It's people who never go anywhere who have the most detailed conceptions of the dangers beyond their door. I've been all over the place, and I've never come across anyone half as dangerous as the Zeds of the world.

MEL: Don't say that.

JONATHAN: Why? What's Zed going to do? If Zed is like any of the other Zeds I've met, he's too busy drooling in his sleep to come out and give me any trouble. He's too busy diddling his uncooperative dick to even step to the window. (*Yelling.*) Right, Zed? You wanna come fight a cripple?

MEL: Stop it!

JONATHAN: (*Yelling.*) Or are you too fat and lazy to step outside?

(Quickly, she's on him -- one hand on his mouth, the knife against his throat.)

MEL: I told you to stop! (*She listens for any sounds in the distance.*) You think you know what you're dealing with? You don't. If Zed were to find you here, he wouldn't politely ask you to leave. Nine months ago, one of his own children came into the world deformed. Healthy, but one of her legs wasn't right. Zed took her into his arms, and, without a word, snapped her neck. That's who Zed is. (*She listens again.*) Now. Are you going to be quiet?

(JONATHAN is still and quiet. She removes her hand from his mouth.)

JONATHAN: Jesus! Yes! Now get the hell off me.

(He pushes her off of him -- and at that moment, realizes the truth about MEL.)

JONATHAN (CONT'D): Oh. Jesus.

MEL: Oh!

(Beat -- both processing this new info.)

JONATHAN: Oh my god! I can't believe I --

(MEL starts to gather her things.)

JONATHAN (CONT'D): Wait -- Don't go. I'm not going to hurt you. Please! Don't go! Please, Mel -- Shit! That's probably not even your name.

(Pause.)

MEL: Melissa.

JONATHAN: What?

MEL: Mel is for Melissa.

JONATHAN: Right. Of course. *(Beat.)* You really had me fooled. *(He looks at her again.)* I mean, I see it, now --

MEL: God... stop.

JONATHAN: I'm sorry, Melissa.

MEL: Don't -- just. Forget it..

(She gets her pack and starts to go.)

JONATHAN: Wait. Melissa --

MEL: I said don't! No one calls me that. No one.

JONATHAN: OK. (*Beat.*) Just -- don't go. I'm no more dangerous now than I was before. I'm a lamb. Trust me.

MEL: (*Shaking her head.*) I've broken enough rules for one night.

JONATHAN: Well, if you're breaking rules, that calls for a celebration!

(*He reaches into his pack to retrieve something.*)

MEL: I'm not 12. It's not like you can --

(*He brings out a small specimen container and opens it for her.*)

MEL (CONT'D): Oh...

JONATHAN: Ta da! (*Beat.*) Come on. Try one.

MEL: What are they?

(*He reaches into the container to show her a small, beautiful berry.*)

JONATHAN: Blackberries. (*Popping it into his mouth and sucking on it.*) Mmmm.

(*He holds out the container, and she kneels near him, reaching in and choosing a single berry. He puts another berry in his mouth, and, finally, she follows suit.*)

MEL: Mmmmm!

JONATHAN: Don't chew. Just suck on it. Push the berry against your teeth to find the seeds. There's... a bunch of them. (*He spits one out onto the tip of his finger to show her.*) Like this. (*She spits a couple of seeds out, carefully.*) There you go. (*Beat.*) So. Tell me. What's wrong with "Melissa"?

MEL: (*Shrugs.*) No one calls me that. Not anymore.

JONATHAN: Okay. You live here?

MEL: Yep. I work here. In the trees. (*Beat.*) Apple. We have a pretty big orchard -- just over that hill.

JONATHAN: He was right!

MEL: Huh?

JONATHAN: Nothing. (*Beat.*) Here: put the seeds in here. (*Holding out the container. Trying a new tactic:*) You work here?

MEL: I'm a pollinator.

JONATHAN: No kidding. Pollination's a hard job. I guess most families need their kids to pitch in.

MEL: This isn't my family.

JONATHAN: Oh. Where's your family?

MEL: Dead.

JONATHAN: Sorry.

MEL: It's OK. (*Beat.*) Seems like a long time ago. My parents were going to take me out of the city when everyone started getting the flux, but then they got sick too --

JONATHAN: I'm sorry, the what?

MEL: The flux. Fever, headaches, these sores all over your body, the coughing... It was awful, how they kept coughing up all this blood. You've never heard of it?

JONATHAN: No, I have. I just... thought it was called something else.

MEL: I tried to take care of them -- but I was just a kid.

JONATHAN: You... took care of them? When they were sick?

MEL: Yeah. Why.

JONATHAN: Nothing. (*Beat.*) So how'd you get out here?

MEL: Well... After my parents died, I didn't know what to do. I stayed in our apartment for a few days -- and then they started to smell. I know, it sounds terrible: I still didn't want to go, but it just smelled... So. I saw a caravan of people leaving the city. I packed as much as I could in these two big suitcases. You should have seen me, dragging these suitcases down the middle of the street. I begged them to let me come with them.

JONATHAN: Where were they going?

MEL: I'm not sure any of them knew, really. Away. Just... away. After a couple of days on the road, I noticed a man in a truck, following us. When we stopped, he said he'd take us to a refugee camp. The next morning, when I woke up, everyone else had gone. It was just me, and the man in the truck. He said everyone else left for the camp, but that he had work for me, if I wanted it. That was Zed. He drove me here. And I've been here ever since.

JONATHAN: So... it's you and Zed?

MEL: And Sarah. And a bunch of little girls.

JONATHAN: No boys?

MEL: (*Shrug.*) Zed says girls are good climbers.

JONATHAN: I guess. (*Beat.*) Maybe when my ankle's better, maybe you can show me the trees.

MEL: No.

JONATHAN: Why not?

MEL: It's not safe.

JONATHAN: Is it safe here?

MEL: Mostly. Well, except for you.

(They smile. MEL eyes the container of berries.)

JONATHAN: Have another. (*She takes one, as does he, and they suck the tart juices from the berries.*) My mother used to talk about my grandmother's stand of blackberries. She used to tell me about being sent out to fetch a pail of berries, and eating twice what she carried back, her fingers stained deep red.

(MEL sucks at her fingertips and rubs her hands on her trousers as JONATHAN spits a few seeds into the container.)

MEL: Why do you want the seeds?

JONATHAN: To save them.

MEL: Why?

JONATHAN: It's what I do. *(Offering the container again.)* Last one.

MEL: I shouldn't. My fingers will give me away.

JONATHAN: *(Laughs.)* You're already given away.

(He shows her his tongue.)

MEL: Shit.

JONATHAN: It's getting dark. No one will see.

(A brief silence. Abruptly, she stands.)

MEL: I should go.

JONATHAN: Oh -- OK. *(Beat.)* Don't forget your book.

MEL: *(Leafing through the pages.)* Why do you have a book about bees?

JONATHAN: I don't know. It smells good. It has nice pictures.

MEL: I can read.

JONATHAN: Of course.

MEL: (*Reading from the table of contents.*) Diseases... enemies of bees... Foulbrood? Pretty gruesome.

JONATHAN: I guess so.

MEL: Sarah says it's punishment.

JONATHAN: Wait -- Who's Sarah?

MEL: Sarah owns this place.

JONATHAN: With Zed.

MEL: Yeah. Sarah says it's God's wrath upon us, that the bees are gone. People worshipped money, and possessions -- we brought it on ourselves. And when we are pure again, she says, they'll return, and we'll be like Moses, in the land of milk and honey.

(Beat.)

JONATHAN: That's the dumbest thing I've ever heard.

MEL: Well --

JONATHAN: The bees left because of some religious imperative? What's next? Locusts? Killing all the first born?

MEL: I didn't say I believed it.

JONATHAN: Really?

MEL: The bees are gone. God or not, they're gone.

JONATHAN: I think it's pretty cowardly to blame it all on God. Or morality. At least, it's cowardly not to admit that we had anything to do with it.

(MEL walks toward her hiding place in the machinery.)

MEL: Do you think they're gone? For good?

JONATHAN: Probably. We probably deserved that.

MEL: Who's getting moral now?

(She slides the book in between two pesticide containers.)

JONATHAN: What are you doing?

MEL: I live with a lot of nosy girls. It'll be safer here.

(The voice on the walkie talkie grumbles.)

MEL (CONT'D): I need to go.

JONATHAN: Really?

MEL: There's always someone calling after me, always something else for me to do -- *(Beat.)* They'll notice.

JONATHAN: I'm sure they will. *(Beat.)* Well, Melissa --

MEL: Mel.

JONATHAN: Mel. Thank you for your kind attention.

MEL: OK. Now remember --

JONATHAN: Stay here, and stay quiet.

MEL: Yes.

JONATHAN: Or Zed will snap my neck.

MEL: It's not a joke.

JONATHAN: Who's joking?

(Pause.)

JONATHAN (CONT'D): See you in the morning?

MEL: ...Maybe.

(JONATHAN watches her leave. And he smiles.)

(SOUND CUE: a cacophony of girls singing and the fuzz and whine of tuning in and out of radio frequencies.)

(Early morning. Somewhere, a single bird calls, repeatedly, for a mate. JONATHAN is sleeping against his pack, while MEL is sitting on an old tractor, reading the book JONATHAN gave her, a small pack next to her. She hears the bird call, and whistles back. This wakes JONATHAN, with a start.)

MEL (CONT'D): 'Morning.

JONATHAN: Jesus! You shouldn't sneak up on a guy.

MEL: I didn't sneak. I walked. I walked in, saw you sleeping, and decided to wait for you to wake up. A guy like you should learn to sleep less soundly.

JONATHAN: I sleep like a new mother. You sneak. I'd bet on it.

(She smiles at this, and puts the book down.)

MEL: I brought you breakfast. And a new bandage for your ankle.

JONATHAN: Are you my protector now?

MEL: I guess so.

(She hands him the sack of food, which he proceeds to devour.)

JONATHAN: Excellent.

MEL: Foot up. Let's fix this.

(During the following, MEL quickly and effectively rewraps his ankle with an ACE bandage.)

JONATHAN: Tomatoes. The breakfast of champeens. You eat a lot of tomatoes around here?

MEL: They're easy. They pretty much take care of themselves, you know.

JONATHAN: What about apples?

MEL: What about 'em?

JONATHAN: You have an orchard full of 'em. Doesn't a guy get an apple, too?

MEL: Those aren't for eating.

JONATHAN: Then... what are they for?

MEL: Selling.

JONATHAN: Are you telling me you don't eat any of them?

MEL: Well, if there's fallen fruit.

JONATHAN: But everything else --

MEL: Zed takes away.

JONATHAN: Well. That's just mean.

MEL: (*She smiles.*) All right. Try that out.

(She returns to the tractor, and JONATHAN tries the new wrap, gingerly walking around the orchard.)

JONATHAN: Hey. That's pretty good.

MEL: You're still limping.

JONATHAN: It hasn't been very long.

MEL: I don't know how you'll make it out of here on foot.

JONATHAN: You thought I walked here?

MEL: What -- you flew?

JONATHAN: No. I have a bike.

MEL: A what?

JONATHAN: Motorcycle.

MEL: You do not.

JONATHAN: I sure do.

MEL: Where is it?

JONATHAN: Nowhere you'll find it. (*Beat.*) See, I'm not totally useless as a man living on his own. I know enough to stow my ride so it's not stolen by ne'er-do-wells like you.

MEL: Well, good for you.

(She goes back to reading, and he goes back to gingerly working out his ankle.)

JONATHAN: I haven't seen anyone else. You sure there's some gang of girls up there?

MEL: Yup.

JONATHAN: Nobody's come down here.

MEL: Nobody's supposed to. The girls stay pretty close to the house.

JONATHAN: You're here.

MEL: I can take care of myself.

JONATHAN: Yes, you can. (*Beat.*) Is that my book?

MEL: My book.

JONATHAN: Right. What do you think?

MEL: Good. It's kinda... sad, though, in a way.

JONATHAN: What do you mean?

MEL: Well, here we are: we've kept bees for -- thousands and thousands of years.

JONATHAN: Well, it's hard to say that we kept them --

MEL: OK, but... even thousands of years ago, they found them, and took them in, the bees.

(She leafs to the section of the book about the Egyptians, and shows it to him.)

MEL (CONT'D): Here. The Egyptians. Did you read this?

JONATHAN: (*Looking at the page. Lying.*) Not really.

MEL: (*Paraphrasing what she sees there.*) Well, they had ways to lure them, to feed them. They had medicines for them -- they knew all this -- and yet... (*Beat.*) What if they're out there? Waiting?

JONATHAN : Waiting for what?

MEL: Us? (*Beat.*) I don't know why I should read all this -- Now, that is. Now that they've all gone. It's like learning a language I'll never speak. Or finding a map to a place that no longer exists.

(She shoves the book back in its hiding place. In doing so, she cuts her hand, slicing the palm deeply.)

MEL (CONT'D): Ah -- shit!

JONATHAN: Let me see that --

MEL: It's just a little scrape.

(He inspects the cut, which is bleeding quite heavily.)

JONATHAN: Man -- you don't do things half way, do you.

MEL: It's OK.

JONATHAN: It's not. Sit.

(She does. He gets his canteen to wash the cut.)

JONATHAN (CONT'D): This is deep. (*Beat. He regards her as he tends to her wound.*) We should sew it up.

MEL: OK.

JONATHAN: It's gonna hurt...

MEL: I don't care.

(He pulls out his first-aid kit, which includes basic suture supplies. He daubs on some disinfectant, etc.)

JONATHAN: You sure? (*She nods.*) Don't look.

MEL: I've seen worse.

(She continues to examine her own cut.)

JONATHAN: Really. Don't look. It'll make me nervous. Talk to me.

MEL: About what?

JONATHAN: I don't know. The orchard. I still wanna see those beautiful trees.

MEL: I told you: That's not safe.

JONATHAN: What about at night?

MEL: Alarms.

JONATHAN: Oh.

(She inhales a bit at the first stitch.)

MEL: You some kind of doctor?

JONATHAN: *(He laughs.)* No. Just a man of many talents.

MEL: Stitching up cuts is a talent?

JONATHAN: Well, it comes in handy in my line of work.

MEL: I thought you were a freeloader.

JONATHAN: No, I'm a gatherer. A collector.

MEL: Of seeds.

JONATHAN: Uh huh.

MEL: And how are you not a freeloader?

JONATHAN: I don't take everything. I replant some seeds there on the spot, and I take samples of the others.

MEL: What's the point of that?

JONATHAN: There are libraries of seeds -- seed banks all over the world, to save what can be saved.

MEL: And who runs that -- the government?

JONATHAN: Which government is that? No, farmers. Scientists.

MEL: You work at a -- library?

JONATHAN: No. I bring my seeds to a lab, where they collect them, catalogue them, and send them to the seed libraries, so that they can be grown, and harvested, and saved again --

MEL: So, you are a thief.

JONATHAN: I prefer to think of myself as a rescuer.

MEL: They wouldn't be able to survive without you?

JONATHAN: They might survive just fine. We, on the other hand --

MEL: What?

JONATHAN: Let's just say we have a lot to learn.

(JONATHAN pauses with the bloody bandana, which he then pockets carefully without letting MEL see.)

MEL: What are you doing here?

JONATHAN: Huh?

MEL: Are you here for seeds?

JONATHAN: *(Lying.)* No, I told you. I got lost. I just -- I got lost, twisted my ankle. Lucky thing I found you.

MEL: Yeah. *(Beat.)* So, you travel a lot.

JONATHAN: I'm always traveling.

MEL: Is it scary -- out there?

JONATHAN: Sometimes it is. It depends on who you meet. Mostly I go where I don't meet anyone. 'Cause, mostly, people suck. *(Beat.)* There's an advantage to living out where everyone else has abandoned hope.

MEL: Why?

JONATHAN: Because that's exactly where you find it. *(Bandage complete.)* Well, you're all done. Keep it clean.

MEL: I will.

(They stand, close enough to kiss. After a moment, JONA- THAN steps back, wobbling a bit on his bad ankle. MEL steadies him, and they laugh.)

JONATHAN: We're a pair, aren't we.

MEL: (*Beat.*) I need to go.

JONATHAN: You just got here.

MEL: But if I'm gone too long --

JONATHAN: You'll be missed. I know.

(*She smiles, and turns to go. Then, she comes back, and quickly kisses him on the cheek.*)

MEL: Thank you.

(*She runs off.*)

JONATHAN: ...You're welcome.

(*After a beat, he goes to his pack, and his phone. He gives it a couple of good cranks.*)

JONATHAN (CONT'D): Yeah. Thomas. I'm sorry to tell you this, man: it's a bust. The orchard you heard about -- All the trees are dead. (*Pause.*) I'm sure that's what they thought -- but -- I'm looking right at 'em. (*Pause*) Yeah. Disappointing. (*Pause.*) Oh, Christ -- no. Don't send Andrew. Yeah, my ankle is fine now. (*Pause.*) No, seriously. I'm fine. I'll keep scouting the area, and let you know if I find anything. Yeah. I'll call. (*Pause.*) I said: I'll call.

(*He hangs up the receiver. Then, he takes out the bloody bandana, which he carefully places in a specimen jar.*)

(*Morning sun -- the farmhouse. DEBORAH is helping to lace up SARAH's shoes. A dress is draped over a chair.*)

SARAH: Not so tight.

DEBORAH: Sorry. (*Regarding the dress.*) That's pretty.

SARAH: Mm hm.

DEBORAH: I've never seen you wear it.

SARAH: I used to. When you were small. When Zed first came here.

DEBORAH: Oh.

(*MEL enters SARAH's room, and appears to be just finished repairing something, screwing something back in place with her knife. Then, SARAH is surprised by a pain in her belly, which she tries to ignore.*)

MEL: Are you just getting dressed?

DEBORAH: Mornings take a little longer these days, OK?

SARAH: Deborah, please. Just a little looser.

(*The pain is stronger, sharper.*)

MEL: Sarah?

SARAH: I'm fine. I'm fine. (*She's not.*) Oh... (*Closing her eyes in response to the pain, breathing more deliberately.*) I can't lose this one, too --

MEL: Sarah, stop. (*Rubbing her lower back to help with the pain.*) Come on, breathe --

SARAH: I am so afraid --

MEL: Sarah, sh...

SARAH: I'm afraid that -- the baby --

DEBORAH: The baby's fine. He's fine.

(Then, the pain subsides.)

SARAH: Oh, praise Jesus. *(Beat.)* Thank you.

(SARAH tries to get up.)

MEL: Wait -- just rest a moment.

SARAH: You, neither of you, must speak of this to Zed. Deborah -- Help me up. *(She does.)* Zed wants a boy. We all want a boy.

DEBORAH: *(To Mel.)* She's been this way all morning.

SARAH: But as for what God wants... I have to trust that somehow these things are for a reason. I can't change what can't be changed. So... Mel?

(SARAH presents the dress to MEL.)

SARAH (CONT'D): This is for you.

MEL: Have you ever seen me where a dress? Let Deborah have it.

DEBORAH: I like the color.

SARAH: No. *(To Mel.)* You need to start looking more like a woman.

MEL: What?

DEBORAH: I think it's pretty.

SARAH: Deborah, quiet. (*To Mel.*) If I lose this baby --

MEL: <u>What</u>?

SARAH: I have to think of the future.

MEL: No...

SARAH: You have to take my place.

MEL: You can't ask me that.

SARAH: I'm not asking you. I am telling you.

MEL: I've done everything you've asked here --

(Overlapping at *.)

SARAH: This is all you have. Your family is dead, and we're your family* now.

MEL: *You're not --

SARAH: We are your family, and you will take your proper place* in it.

MEL: *My proper -- ?

SARAH: The world may sink into decay, it may collapse on the weight of its *misery --

MEL: *I'm not going to --

(SARAH strikes her, hard.)

SARAH: You will do as I say. You must destroy the past, Mel. To be free, you must leave it all behind. (*Handing her the dress, almost sweetly.*) Be cheerful, Mel. You will have such beautiful babies.

(*SARAH exits, followed quickly by DEBORAH, MEL left, stunned, with the dress.*)

(*Cross fade, as MEL walks slowly back into the orchard. JONATHAN and all his things are gone.*)

MEL: Jonathan?

DEBORAH (O.S.): Mel, wait --

MEL: Go away.

DEBORAH: (*Entering.*) Mel! What's the matter?

MEL: Deborah, not now.

DEBORAH: You must have known --

MEL: What?

DEBORAH: (*Beat.*) You didn't even guess, did you?

MEL: No.

DEBORAH: My mother's getting too old for babies. That's no secret.

MEL: The baby is fine...

DEBORAH: The last one wasn't.

MEL: So?

DEBORAH: So -- you've been chosen. To tell you the truth, I don't think you deserve it. And don't think that you're taking her place. You'll be the womb, but they'll still be her babies. So, how's that make you feel? You talk a lot about following the rules... but what about now, Mel? How do you feel about doing what he says now?

MEL: Stop.

DEBORAH: Are you ready to have his hands on you?

MEL: I'll kill him if he tries.

DEBORAH: He'll kill you first. (*Beat.*) I know: you should just leave. You just leave that with me, and run. I'll never tell them.

(DEBORAH holds out her hand for the dress.)

MEL: You know there's nowhere for me to go.

DEBORAH: (*Beat.*) I thought you were braver than that.

(DEBORAH exits. When Mel is sure she's gone, she takes off her clothing, stripping down to her underwear and holds up the dress in front of her. Disgusted, she rolls up the dress, and goes to the tractor to put the dress in her hiding place.)

(Then, she sees the book, and pulls it out. She sits with it, and flips through the pages. Then, she hits upon a section that gives her pause.)

MEL: (*Reading.*) "Age of Bees. It may be rather difficult to decide how long a worker bee would live if kept from wearing itself out by active labors of the fields..."

(As she reads, we see a single blossom appearing in her tree. In a pool of light, we see DEBORAH tending to Sarah, braiding her hair, lovingly.)

MEL (CONT'D): (*Continuing to read from the book.*) "During the summer months the life of the worker bees is cut short by the wearing out of its wings, and at the close of a warm day, hundreds of these heavily-laden, ragged-winged veterans will be found making their way into the hives slowly and painfully as compared with the nimble and perfect-winged young bees."

(DEBORAH continues to tend to SARAH.)

MEL (CONT'D): (*Continuing to read.*) "If the ground around the apiary is examined at nightfall, numbers of these old bees may be seen hopping about, evidently recognizing their own inability to be of further use to the community..."

(MEL drops the book, and picks up the dress again.)

MEL (CONT'D): I must be nimble and perfect winged...

(She begins to put on the dress, but it is shameful and difficult.)

(As she dresses, JONATHAN enters, packed to leave. He is limping only slightly. He watches her dress, and takes a few beats to look at the oddly clad figure in the orchard. Then, it dawns on him.)

JONATHAN: Mel?

(She is surprised, and turns to shove her old clothing into the tractor.)

JONATHAN (CONT'D): I'm sorry -- I didn't mean to... *(Beat.)* I'm sorry.

(She picks up the book, and makes herself as small as possible. A pause.)

JONATHAN (CONT'D): I have to head out. I was worried that I wouldn't see you again. I figured I'd just have to wait for a while, or leave you a note for the next time you decide to come out to read, or whatever it is you do out here. *(Beat.)* You OK? Mel?

(After a moment.)

MEL: Do you ever catch yourself going along, doing nothing out of the ordinary, when it's suddenly like you're trapped in someone else's body, like these hands aren't your hands, and how strange it is that you're seeing out of these eyes, and you think, how odd, that I'm me... that in this weird accident of birth, I was put in this body. For a moment, it's as if you're coming out of a dream, but still caught in it, and it's terrifying that you'll never completely wake from it. You're trapped, and you can't move, and you can't understand how you got here. You want to scream, but this voice isn't your voice, and you want to run, but these aren't your legs -- and, anyway, if you were to run, where would you go? You wait for the dream to dissolve, but it doesn't. And, just as suddenly, you realize: no, this is real. This is never going to end.

JONATHAN: Hey...

MEL: Don't -- (*Beat.*) It's nothing. Please.

JONATHAN: If you say so. But I think I'll just sit here for a minute to make sure.

MEL: You don't need to.

JONATHAN: I think I will anyway.

MEL: (*Beat.*) I thought you'd already gone.

JONATHAN: Nope.

MEL: You should go.

JONATHAN: Why?

MEL: There's nothing good here.

JONATHAN: I wouldn't say that.

(He smiles at her.)

MEL: What.

JONATHAN: It's a good color for you. You look nice. In that color.

MEL: I don't.

JONATHAN: Well, it's just a little funny to see you dressed like that --

(She's begun to cry.)

JONATHAN (CONT'D): Oh, god... What did I say? I'm a dope. I'm sorry.

MEL: No, I'm fine.

JONATHAN: I didn't mean anything --

MEL: It's OK.

JONATHAN: It's a nice dress.

MEL: It's not.

(He kisses her, gently.)

MEL (CONT'D): I'm glad you stayed.

JONATHAN: Me too.

(Then, she sees the blossom in the tree.)

MEL: Oh!

JONATHAN: What?

MEL: Look at that. (*Regarding the tree.*) It's blooming...

JONATHAN: And you thought these were dead.

MEL: They are.

JONATHAN: This one clearly isn't -- well, not quite.

MEL: It's just a fluke.

JONATHAN: Maybe. (*Beat.*) Come on! Let's make an apple.

MEL: I don't see the point.

JONATHAN: There has to be a point? Come on. Teach me how to pollinate.

(He begins climbing.)

MEL: Careful -- your ankle.

JONATHAN: My ankle's fine. Come on.

MEL: You know a little about it, right?

JONATHAN: Pollination? Well, let's consider me a rank beginner.

(He's reached the blossom, and clings there, balancing on one foot.)

MEL: OK. When an apple blossoms, OK ... Some plants, you can just shake 'em, and the fruit will grow. Not apples. They're not -- what's the word -- they're not self-pollinating.

JONATHAN: I know that part.

MEL: Well, hold on. The pollen has to come from a different tree, and it's not gonna happen with a big gust of wind. *(Goes to her pack, fishes out a small cheesecloth bag with apple blossoms from another tree.)* So we have a system of having other pollinators --

JONATHAN: This lecture going to take long?

MEL: It's important. *(Throws him the bag of blossoms.)* These are from the crab-apples in the late blossoming trees.

JONATHAN: They smell nice.

MEL: It gets old. OK. Get the crab blossom ready. You pinch the petals back. Hold on. Throw me one.

JONATHAN: OK. (*He does.*)

MEL: Now watch me. (*She pulls back the petals to expose the stamen of the flower.*) Just like this. (*Pointing inside of the flower.*) See these sticky outy bits --

JONATHAN: The anther?

MEL: I dunno. The long yellow bits. They've got all the pollen on 'em. And the pollen has to get into the other blossom.

JONATHAN: Right.

MEL: Watch. Pretend my hand here is a blossom. (*She models the quick dusting of anther to stigma, swirling the blossom in the center of her fist.*) You just -- swirl it, kind of, to get the pollen in there. Got it?

(*He does as she instructs.*)

JONATHAN: Got it.

MEL: And -- that's it.

JONATHAN: And now?

MEL: And now we wait.

JONATHAN: And now we wait. (*He carefully lowers himself from the tree.*) How long?

MEL: In a few weeks, you'll see the blossom start to swell. With a bloom this late, the apples would be ready in September.

JONATHAN: I'll have to be back for the harvest, then.

(Unseen, DEBORAH comes back to the orchard. She stops at a safe distance, and watches MEL with this strange man.)

MEL: You have to go?

JONATHAN: Yeah. There's something important I have to do. They're expecting me.

MEL: Who?

JONATHAN: I'll come back. I promise. But right now -- I need to head out.

(A short pause.)

MEL: Take me.

JONATHAN: ...What?

MEL: Take me with you.

JONATHAN: Oh... hey...

MEL: Couldn't I help you? I could find seeds. I could travel --

JONATHAN: That's not a great idea.

MEL: Why?

JONATHAN: It's not safe.

MEL: I know -- but I'd be with you.

JONATHAN: I think Zed might have something to say about this.

MEL: I don't care.

JONATHAN: And the people I know -- I have to make arrangements. I can't just show up with you.

MEL: Why not?

JONATHAN: There are things I need to do. You understand, right? It's not safe to just -- walk out of here, unprepared. So let me go, now. And then... I'll come back.

MEL: No, you won't.

JONATHAN: I have to. I want to see what happens with our apple.

MEL: Forget it.

JONATHAN: I'll come back. As soon as I can. Or, at least, by September.

(He kisses her.)

MEL: September.

(And he's gone. DEBORAH steps out from the shadows.)

DEBORAH: Who was that?

MEL: Deborah! You shouldn't be here.

(MEL goes to the sensors to fiddle with wiring, as if that's what's she been doing here.)

DEBORAH: Well, you shouldn't be here either, I don't think. Alone or otherwise.

MEL: Go back to the house.

DEBORAH: He's handsome. Who is he?

MEL: No one.

DEBORAH: It seemed to me that you knew him.

MEL: He was no one.

DEBORAH: I think Sarah would be very interested to know that you're speaking with strange men out here. She'd find that very interesting indeed.

MEL: There's nothing to tell.

DEBORAH: I think Zed would be very interested in this as well.

MEL: Listen to me, Deborah. I have more than a few secrets of yours. I'll tell them about the times you sneak off to the cold cellars to sleep. I'll tell them about the little things you've stolen and kept secret behind the floor board in your room. The long hours you spend swimming in the river, of the chores you pawn off to others -- If you say one word about Jonathan, I'll tell them all of it.

DEBORAH: *(After a beat.)* So. He has a name.

MEL: Not one word.

DEBORAH: Fine. Not a word.

(Deborah starts to leave the orchard, and then pauses.)

DEBORAH (CONT'D): Will it be hard to wait -- for September?

(DEBORAH exits. MEL turns to look at the blossom on the tree as the lights fade.)

END OF ACT.

ACT TWO

(An early autumn morning. SARAH sleeps in her rocking chair. Her pregnancy has progressed, and it's nearly time for her to give birth.)

(In another room, DEBORAH undresses -- smiling to an unseen individual.)

(In the orchard, we see MEL's tree, and the blossom that has fattened into a healthy, vibrant apple.)

(Just outside the orchard, JONATHAN kneels by his pack, dials in a new frequency, and cranks his field telephone a few times.)

JONATHAN: I'm calling for Dr. Freeman. (*Pause.*) What? (*Pause.*) Oh -- Yes. The code. Hold on... (*Reading a code written on his hand.*) Echo zulu 7-9-5 bravo. (*Pause.*) OK. Well, I need to speak with the Dr. -- (*Pause.*) Oh -- My name is Jonathan -- (*Pause.*) Right. The one with the blood sample. (*Pause.*) "The subject....?" She has a name, for god's sake.

(MEL appears at the edge of the orchard. She is still wearing a dress, and does so more easily than before. Her hair is, perhaps, a bit longer, and there is something more softly feminine -- though not overtly sexual or "girly" -- about her appearance. She listens while JONATHAN continues to speak on the telephone.)

JONATHAN (CONT'D): Yeah, I know you'd like to move fast. The samples are important, earth-shattering, all that. I understand. It's just -- It isn't exactly painless. And the situation -- it's not without its dangers. So before the next step -- (*Pause.*) It's just -- I want reassur-

69

ances that -- (*Pause.*) Maybe I should speak with the doctor himself, huh? (*Beat.*) Well, when will he be able to speak with me? (*Pause.*) Tomorrow? Jesus! (*Pause.*) Fine. I'll call tomorrow. (*Pause.*) Shit!

(JONATHAN hangs up the phone, and turns to enter the orchard.)

MEL: Wait!

JONATHAN: (*Surprised.*) Mel!

MEL: Don't move...

(She scrambles up the nearest sensor unit, and disables something.)

MEL (CONT'D): OK. Now you can come in. (*Beat.*) Alarms.

JONATHAN: There wasn't an alarm last time.

MEL: Last time you were lucky.

JONATHAN: What if you hadn't caught me? What if Zed --

MEL: He's gone. I would have told Sarah the sensors malfunctioned.

(She gestures for him to enter, which he does, somewhat carefully.)

JONATHAN: Zed's gone.

MEL: To the trader.

JONATHAN: Well.

MEL: I wasn't sure if I'd see you again.

JONATHAN: I told you I'd be back.

MEL: It's been a long time.

JONATHAN: Yeah.

(They pause, smiling.)

MEL: I have a surprise for you.

(The apple.)

JONATHAN: Hey! We did it!

MEL: Uh huh.

JONATHAN: It's a beauty. What kind is it?

MEL: I'm not sure. A Chessen King...? Crimson King? I
    can't remember.

(He goes to pick it.)

MEL (CONT'D): No! Not yet.

(She goes to him, and kisses him.)

MEL (CONT'D): Not yet.

*(He kisses her back. Their embrace is immediately, sur-
prisingly, passionate.)*

(Lights cross fade to DEBORAH, tiptoeing into SARAH's room. Sees her sleeping in the chair, and walks very quietly over to SARAH's dresser, and tries to open the drawers as quietly as possible.)

SARAH: *(Rousing.)* Zed?

DEBORAH: *(Closing the drawer.)* No, Mother.

SARAH: What's wrong?

DEBORAH: Nothing. You go back to sleep.

SARAH: I wasn't really sleeping. I don't sleep, actually, these days. If I move, the baby sleeps; If I sleep, the baby thrashes like he's trying to kick his way out.

DEBORAH: Can I feel it?

SARAH: He's not moving, now.

DEBORAH: Better sleep while you can, then.

(SARAH closes her eyes, and DEBORAH hangs back, watching her. SARAH sighs.)

SARAH: Deborah ...?

DEBORAH: Yes? Would you like some tea?

SARAH: No.

DEBORAH: Something to eat then.

SARAH: Oh, stop. *(Beat.)* If you're staying, get my book.

(DEBORAH gets a well-worn Bible from one of the drawers.)

SARAH (CONT'D): Come on. Read to me a bit.

(DEBORAH sits with the book, and leafs through the first pages.)

DEBORAH: Who was Jenny, again?

SARAH: Your great-grandmother. That was hers, remember?

DEBORAH: And Jenny took you to the place where they all read the book together?

SARAH: To church. And no. My mother took me. And there wasn't just reading. We would sing, and the preacher gave a lesson.

DEBORAH: About what?

SARAH: About something from the book.

DEBORAH: Like what kinds of lessons?

SARAH: I don't remember everything, Deborah. I was very young.

DEBORAH: Tell me about the tongues of fire.

SARAH: Again?

DEBORAH: I like that part.

SARAH: Well, it didn't happen to everyone. I just remember, we'd be praying, and singing, and then, it was like someone was taken up, like something entered into a person, and they spoke a language we didn't understand -- And the rest would call out, weep -- it was a joyous thing.

DEBORAH: And if you don't have tongues of fire?

SARAH: Then you speak quietly to God, in your own words. He'll hear.

DEBORAH: Everything?

SARAH: Everything. You open your heart, and pray.

DEBORAH: For what?

SARAH: Strength. Patience...

DEBORAH: Not for things. But... for a baby?

SARAH: Yes, of course. (*Beat.*) Read to me.

DEBORAH: (*Sighs.*)

SARAH: Deborah. Go to Revelation. Where it's marked.

(*DEBORAH turns the page, reluctantly, as SARAH closes her eyes.*)

DEBORAH: (*Somewhat slowly.*) "Remember therefore how thou hast received and heard, and hold fast, and repent. If therefore thou shalt not watch, I will come upon thee as a thief, and thou shalt not know what hour I will come upon thee..."

(Cross fade to the orchard.)

(MEL and JONATHAN sit under the tree, partially undressed, his head in her lap. His finger traces the scar on her palm where her cut has mostly healed. He looks up at her.)

JONATHAN: Mel, I need to ask you something --

MEL: Shhh.

JONATHAN: It's important.

MEL: Right.

JONATHAN: If you could have saved your parents, what would you have done?

MEL: What are you talking about?

JONATHAN: I mean, if you could have done something to save them, you would have done it, right?

MEL: Sure. Of course.

JONATHAN: So -- what if it was someone else's parents? What would you do to save them?

MEL: This is depressing.

JONATHAN: No, listen. What if someone told you that you could do something?

MEL: Jonathan, what does it matter?

JONATHAN: Hear me out: I have a question.

MEL: No -- I should be asking <u>you</u> questions.

JONATHAN: Mel --

MEL: I don't know anything about you.

JONATHAN: Sure you do.

MEL: You travel alone. You find seeds. You bring them... somewhere.

JONATHAN: That's pretty much it.

MEL: That can't be it.

(Brief pause.)

JONATHAN: OK. Fine. Ask.

MEL: Anything?

JONATHAN: Anything.

MEL: OK. (*Beat.*) OK: Where did you come from?

JONATHAN: From the guys with the seeds.

MEL: I mean -- originally.

JONATHAN: What? That's boring.

MEL: No, it's not. (*Beat.*) Really.

JONATHAN: OK... Well. I grew up in a town called Nelson. It was tiny. When I was about 10, my parents sent me away to school -- Nelson didn't have a school. I was away, for a long time... and then one day a letter came saying that my parents had died, and I'd need to leave.

MEL: They died?

JONATHAN: A lot of people died.

MEL: But -- what happened to them?

JONATHAN: Fevers. Sores. Coughing up blood...

MEL: (*Understanding this, fully.*) Oh.

JONATHAN: I went back to Nelson, but the house had been burned down. (He takes out a watch from his pocket, hands it to her.) This was my father's. It's all I have of him.

(She holds the watch for a moment, and returns it to him.)

MEL: I want to show you something.

(She goes to the tractor, and opens the hatch. She pulls out a few pesticide containers.)

MEL (CONT'D): When I left home, I packed some clothing, some food -- and these. (*Opening the lids of a few containers.*) It seems stupid, now. I didn't take any pictures. Just books.

(She pulls out several books.)

JONATHAN: Holy christ...

MEL: Sarah took most of them away -- she said they might carry some sickness. And besides, she said, it wasn't good to keep reminding myself of my parents. I didn't care. I wanted to be reminded. So, I managed to steal these back.

JONATHAN: Nordic history... Gardening... the Brothers Grimm... Shakespeare!

MEL: These books. That's all I have of my parents.

JONATHAN: (*Having opened the cover of one.*) "To Michael, on our 10th anniversary --"

(She reaches out to cover the inscription.)

MEL: Don't do that.

JONATHAN: I'm sorry.

MEL: It's OK.

JONATHAN: (*Pointing to another container.*) What's in that?

MEL: Nothing.

(JONATHAN goes to the container, and opens it before she can stop him.)

JONATHAN: What the --

(He takes out a few pages of material -- scraps of newsprint, magazines, etc.)

MEL: It's nothing.

JONATHAN: Look at all this junk!

MEL: It's not junk.

(She tries to take the scraps out of his hands, and stuffs them back in the container.)

JONATHAN: Where'd it all come from?

MEL: On the wind. Down the creek. From the back of Zed's hauler. Zed brings our fruit to a trader every few weeks, and when he comes back, there are sometimes little scraps tucked between the boxes. I don't know where they come from. Well, it doesn't matter, I guess. I just like to read them.

JONATHAN: Why?

MEL: Sometimes I read them and think how lucky I am to be here, and not out there. Sometimes... I like to know that someone else is out there. That someone's surviving.

JONATHAN: *(Looking at the one still in his hand.)* Someone is. And relatively close, too.

MEL: Huh?

JONATHAN: *(Showing her.)* See?

MEL: *(Shrugging.)* I don't know what that means.

JONATHAN: *(Going to his pack, pulls out his maps, and unfolds a couple.)* Well, here. I'll show you. *(Smooths out one.)* OK. It's not that far...

MEL: What are all those lines?

JONATHAN: Elevations. (*Beat.*) These are topographic maps. The lines show a change in altitude, which is handy if you want to know if your path will take you up and down hills all day.

MEL: Oh.

JONATHAN: (*Going back to the map.*) Let's see... Right: These Vees here? This is your valley.

MEL: (*Looking more carefully.*) It is? I'm right here?

JONATHAN: Yep.

MEL: It's marked. (*Beat.*) You circled it.

JONATHAN: (*Lying.*) After I found you. So I could find you again.

MEL: Right.

JONATHAN: And that paper... is from this town. (*Pointing to the city on an adjacent map.*) Well, when it was a town. I'm not sure who lives there now. I mean, that was printed not too long ago, so there must be someone there.

MEL: (*Pointing at another part of the map.*) What are all these Xs?

JONATHAN: An X marks a place where I've been where -- where it's a deadzone.

MEL: So what's over here, with all these symbols?

JONATHAN: That's better habitat. (*Pointing them out.*)
Aster, currant, snowberry, goldenrod, lupine, sage, lilac
--

MEL: Habitat for what?

(Beat. JONATHAN folds up the map, regretting what he's said.)

MEL (CONT'D): Habitat for <u>what</u>?

JONATHAN: Just -- habitat.

MEL: Wait...

(MEL quickly goes to the "bee" book, and leafs through pages, with mounting excitement.)

JONATHAN: Hold on...

MEL: All those plants -- (*She looks up at him, a revelation.*) You found them?

JONATHAN: I didn't say that.

MEL: You said habitat --

JONATHAN: And even if I did find an isolated colony, I'm not sure I'd tell anybody.

MEL: Why?

JONATHAN: To keep them safe. They're better off on their own.

(A brief pause.)

MEL: I know what you want to ask.

JONATHAN: What?

MEL: What you want. I heard you. On that thing.

JONATHAN: I should explain.

MEL: You need samples of the trees.

JONATHAN: Oh --

MEL: I could get you seeds.

JONATHAN: No. Besides, seeds are a crapshoot. For apples, anyway. I mean, I could take the seeds from a Granny Smith, plant 'em, but I wouldn't get a Granny Smith tree. I might not even get edible fruit. But let's say you have a Winesap tree, and I want to plant a Winesap myself -- well, in order to do that --

MEL: You need grafts from a Winesap. (*Beat.*) How many?

(She gets her knife.)

JONATHAN: Mel --

MEL: Why not?

JONATHAN: I don't want any trouble for you.

MEL: I've got a reason to be in the trees.

JONATHAN: No, you can't --

MEL: I can be brave, like you.

JONATHAN: Mel --

MEL: I can.

JONATHAN: Jesus. (*Smiles.*) Fine. You need to get younger, greener branch --

MEL: I've done grafts. I know what to do. (*Beat.*) You'll see. I'll be good to have around.

(Pause.)

MEL (CONT'D): I'd do anything.

JONATHAN: What?

MEL: You asked what I'd do. If I could have saved them. (*Beat.*) I'd have done anything.

(She smiles, and exits. JONATHAN sits propped against the tree.)

JONATHAN: Jesus. Jesus...

(He rubs his eyes, and holds his head for a moment. Then, DEBORAH enters.)

DEBORAH: I remember you!

(She has startled him, but he tries not to show it.)

DEBORAH (CONT'D): It's been a long time, but here you are! (*Beat.*) I see it.

JONATHAN: Uh...

DEBORAH: I can see why she likes you.

JONATHAN: I'm sorry?

DEBORAH: I'm Deborah.

JONATHAN: OK.

DEBORAH: I know who you are!

JONATHAN: You do.

DEBORAH: You're Jonathan.

JONATHAN: (*Beat.*) <u>Who</u> are you?

DEBORAH: <u>Deborah</u>.

JONATHAN: Right.

DEBORAH: I'm like her sister. I mean, we're not sisters. We don't look anything alike, of course. I mean, look at me. Look at her. (*Beat.*) I'm the oldest here. Well, not counting Mel. But she doesn't really count. Not really.

(DEBORAH gets closer to him.)

DEBORAH (CONT'D): I saw you together, once, you know. And I asked her about you, but she just lied. Like I can't tell when she's lying... So, how long are you here, Jonathan?

JONATHAN: I'm just travelling.

DEBORAH: Travelling where?

JONATHAN: Look --

(He pushes himself away from her.)

DEBORAH: I was wondering when we'd see you again. It's been a long time since anyone's come here. I was starting to think that there was no one else in the world. Just us. Me, Zed, Sarah. I've run away before and I've never seen another soul for miles and miles -- so then when you showed up... well, that was a nice surprise.

JONATHAN: OK.

DEBORAH: For some of us.

JONATHAN: Well. It was very nice to meet you --

(He goes to his pack.)

DEBORAH: You're going already?

JONATHAN: Yes.

DEBORAH: Have you seen Mel? Because you wouldn't leave without seeing Mel.

JONATHAN: I wouldn't?

DEBORAH: Why else would you come?

(She is quite close to him now. There is something both seductive and desperate in her approach.)

DEBORAH (CONT'D): But... you wanna know something about Mel...?

JONATHAN: Deborah --

DEBORAH: She doesn't know what I know.

JONATHAN: I really have to go.

DEBORAH: Zed hasn't touched her, you know. I think...
she doesn't understand him. I think she doesn't want to.
I'm prettier than Mel, aren't I?

JONATHAN: Yes, you're a very pretty girl --

*(He tries, again, to push her away, but she clings more
tightly.)*

DEBORAH: I'm a woman!

JONATHAN: OK. You're a woman.

DEBORAH: More woman than Mel.

JONATHAN: I really need to go.

DEBORAH: You don't want her, do you?

*(A walkie talkie in DEBORAH's satchel squawks, a man's
voice calls her name.)*

DEBORAH (CONT'D): He's back. (*Beat.*) He needs me.

*(She turns off the walkie, smiles at him, presses more
closely to him.)*

JONATHAN: OK.

DEBORAH: But I could come back, if you like.

JONATHAN: I don't.

DEBORAH: Yes, you do. You're thinking about me already. You know how I can tell? When a man is flushed, and can hardly look me in the eye. I can practically read your thoughts.

(MEL approaches the orchard, sees DEBORAH and freezes.)

JONATHAN: You're mistaken.

DEBORAH: No, I'm not. I never am.

(DEBORAH kisses him, and he responds momentarily to this seduction before pushing her away. She laughs, and runs off. Then, MEL comes into the orchard. She has a small bundle of cuttings. She is speechless.)

JONATHAN: You got them. Great.

(He goes to his pack, but she just watches him -- hurt and angry.)

JONATHAN (CONT'D): I hope I have something to wrap them --

(She tosses them at him.)

MEL: Just -- Just take them.

JONATHAN: Hey!

MEL: You got what you want -- right?

JONATHAN: What?

MEL: There are your samples. Take them and go.

(He takes them out, and gently checks them, wraps the ends in a cloth.)

JONATHAN: Mel.

MEL: That's _not_ what you want? What _do_ you want, Jonathan?

JONATHAN: What's the matter with you?

MEL: Tell me, Jonathan. Why are you really here? For these cuttings? For... what?

JONATHAN: For you, of course.

MEL: For me.

JONATHAN: Yes.

MEL: Then what about Deborah?

JONATHAN: Oh.

MEL: I saw you.

JONATHAN: It's not what you think.

MEL: You kissed her.

JONATHAN: What do you want me to say --

MEL: Were you going to -- with Deborah? Were you going to --

JONATHAN: Jesus! No!

MEL: For months, I waited --

JONATHAN: I am sorry --

MEL: I thought you'd come back, and then I'd go away with you --

JONATHAN: Yes! Yes.

MEL: That I'd finally leave here, with you --

JONATHAN: If you want to leave, we'll leave. We can do that. (*Beat.*) But there's something I want you to do for me.

MEL: There's something more you want from me?

JONATHAN: Listen --

MEL: Forget it.

JONATHAN: No! Listen! (*Beat.*) The thing that killed your parents? Here's the thing: Anyone who got infected, got the disease. Anyone who got the disease, died.

MEL: A lot of people died.

JONATHAN: Except you. You watched them get sick, but you were OK. You survived.

MEL: So what?

JONATHAN: So what? (*Beat.*) There's something in your blood. You have some ... antibody. Some immunity. There are doctors who are trying to find a cure -- and they want to find out what that is. Of course, they'll need to do blood and marrow samples to confirm it, do some tests to see if a vaccine is possible.

(Pause.)

MEL: That's -- I don't believe you.

JONATHAN: There could be a cure. Because of you.

MEL: Wait... The samples. When I heard you, talking --
The samples: that was about me?

JONATHAN: Yes.

MEL: So, all your talk about seeds -- that was all a lie?

JONATHAN: Of course not!

MEL: Wait! How do you even know this? Did someone
send you here?

JONATHAN: No! When I came here, I was just looking
for trees. I was just told there were trees. That's all. I
didn't even know there'd be people here.

MEL: So how do you know --

JONATHAN: You told me about your parents. You said
you watched them die, and I'd never heard of anyone --
I mean, that's just not possible. So: I brought in your
blood sample--

MEL: What?

JONATHAN: From your cut.

MEL: Oh my god...

JONATHAN: Do you see?

(Longer pause.)

JONATHAN (CONT'D): I can take you away.

MEL: Stop it!

JONATHAN: Aren't you listening? I can take you.

MEL: If you think I'll go anywhere with you, you're crazy.

JONATHAN: You're angry. *(Beat.)* I'll wait. I'll wait right here until you change your mind.

MEL: You'll wait.

JONATHAN: Yes.

MEL: *(Beat.)* That doesn't seem like a very good idea. Deborah knows about you now. Do you trust her to keep her mouth shut about you? Don't you think she'll tell Zed?

JONATHAN: I don't give a fuck about Zed. I can take care of Zed. *(Beat.)* Mel. Please. *(Beat.)* You wanted to leave with me. You said so yourself.

MEL: That was before.

JONATHAN: Before what?

MEL: When I thought I could trust you.

JONATHAN: You can trust me. Please let me take you.

MEL: Where? To do what?

JONATHAN: It's just some tests --

MEL: Just some tests!

JONATHAN: What do you want me to say?

MEL: I -- can't. I can't go.

JONATHAN: You'll stay here.

MEL: Yes.

JONATHAN: With everything you know --

MEL: Yes!

JONATHAN: You'd rather stay here with some psycho-
path --

MEL: Zed will never hurt me!

JONATHAN: Oh, no -- of course not!

MEL: Not with all the healthy babies I'll have.

(A pause while JONATHAN takes that in.)

JONATHAN: ...What?

MEL: You see? He'd never hurt me.

JONATHAN: This is crazy. You're coming with me.

MEL: No, I'm not.

JONATHAN: We need you.

MEL: <u>We</u> need you...?

JONATHAN: I need you.

MEL: Go!

JONATHAN: Mel, please --

MEL: Get out!

(He steps closer to her, but she pulls her knife on him.)

MEL (CONT'D): Get. Out. And I don't want you to ever come back.

JONATHAN: OK... OK. (*Picking up his pa*ck.) I wasn't trying to fool you. Or hurt you. I was trying to protect you. No matter what you think, I can tell you that's true.

(JONATHAN exits. After a beat, MEL rips off her dress, stripping down to her undergarments. She sits, defeated. Then, DEBORAH enters the orchard.)

DEBORAH: What are you doing? Sarah's looking for you.

(Pause. MEL does not respond.)

DEBORAH (CONT'D): Put your clothes on and let's go.

(DEBORAH picks up the dress and holds it out to her.)

DEBORAH (CONT'D): Come on, Mel.

(MEL looks at the dress.)

MEL: You should take that.

DEBORAH: Mel --

MEL: You want it, right? So have it.

DEBORAH: What?

MEL: I don't need it anymore -- not where I'm going.

DEBORAH: Where are you going?

MEL: (*Shrugs*)

DEBORAH: What am I going to tell Sarah?

MEL: I don't know. You decide. Tell her whatever you
like. Now go. (*Beat.*) Now!

*(DEBORAH takes the dress, and exits. MEL gets her pack
from the tractor and begins to pull out her belongings.
She pulls out the container with her scraps of paper --
which she opens, and the papers slowly spill to the
ground, and she watches them fall.)*

*(Cross fade to DEBORAH, putting on MEL's dress. DEB-
ORAH bundles up her old clothing, and stuffs it under the
dress, admiring this swollen belly. SARAH enters.)*

SARAH: Deborah, Zed needs help with the trailer --
(*Seeing her.*) Deborah.

(DEBORAH takes out the padding, quickly.)

DEBORAH: It fits.

SARAH: That belongs to Mel.

DEBORAH: She doesn't want it.

SARAH: Well, you'll give it back.

DEBORAH: No.

SARAH: You're being foolish.

DEBORAH: Zed will like me in this.

SARAH: That is foolishness --

DEBORAH: He loves me!

SARAH: It's not your place!

DEBORAH: It's already my place!

SARAH: (*Overlapping*) Stop it!

DEBORAH: It's been my place for --

SARAH: (*Grabs her arm, more despondent than angry.*) You don't know what you're saying. Now you're giving that back to Mel.

DEBORAH: Mel's gone! She's run away, Mother. And I'm glad to see her go.

(SARAH shoves her daughter, hard.)

SARAH: What? (*Beat.*) What have you done... What have you done?

(DEBORAH gasps and grabs her mother, struck by an intense and blinding headache. She trembles, and speaks in a voice that isn't her own. During the following, SARAH tries to get away, but can't free herself from DEBORAH's grasp.)

DEBORAH: (*It begins quietly, but grows into a pitched frenzy.*) They have been hidden, kept secret, in the wilderness, in the wilderness, calling, calling for salvation, waiting for -- This is the end time the time of glory the time of THEY WILL COME TO RUIN AND TO PUNISH and in the unknown world they will find sanctuary from those who would from those who would -- THEY WILL COME IN FIRE ON THE WIND -- and they will reveal themselves and the world will be --

(*DEBORAH seems to wake, as if coming out of a dream -- now confronted with the troubling vision she now remembers, as well as the reality of her mother's labor, which has commenced, painfully.*)

(*Cross fade to the orchard, where MEL is sitting amidst the clippings and fragments on news, gathering them back up, holding them to her chest. A clipping in her hand catches her eye.*)

MEL: "...Infected persons have been quarantined -- Infections are currently not responding to any known antibiotic..."

(*She laughs and crumples the papers, gathers them into a ragged ball.*)

(*DEBORAH re-enters, panicked. At her appearance, MEL drops the pages, and begins, quickly to dress in her old clothing. She has no patience or kindness for DEBORAH.*)

DEBORAH: Mel! Please -- It's Sarah. I need you --

MEL: What.

DEBORAH: The baby.

MEL: Yes?

DEBORAH: It's time!

MEL: She's done it before.

DEBORAH: This is different. She's started bleeding -- a
lot --

MEL: Then you'd better go!

DEBORAH: I don't know what to do!

MEL: You stand there, and watch it happen.

(MEL hands DEBORAH the knife.)

MEL (CONT'D): You'll need this. For the cord.

DEBORAH: Mel --

MEL: You'd better run, before they both die.

(This hurts. A pause, and then DEBORAH exits.)

*(MEL has finished dressing. She goes to pack the rest of
the belongings, pulls out everything, including all her parents books, for a moment, it seems as if she will pack them
but then she takes one of the books, cracks the spine and
begins to pull pages from the book -- it is both painful and
liberating, and she destroys the book with a kind of aban-
don, scattering the pages in a defiant, desperate farewell.)*

*(She goes to the tractor to pull out anything else she could
pack, and finds the small transistor radio, she switches it
on, and turns the dial, though all she can find is fuzz and
whine of very distant transmissions. During the following,*

a cacophony of sounds fills the air: various indistinct voices from the walkie talkie, the shouting and singing of girls, SARAH's groans and cries of labor --)

MEL (CONT'D): Please -- someone -- anyone ... Please be out there.

(The sounds grow in intensity and volume until it cuts off, abruptly, leaving only an indistinct hum of electronics, or insects.)

MEL (CONT'D): Please: tell me where to go.

(She switches off the radio, drops it, helplessly. Seeing Jonathan's book in the wreckage, she carefully stows it and the radio in her pack.)

(Then, JONATHAN enters the orchard.)

JONATHAN: OK. Fuck it. I don't care what you say --

(Speechless, he takes in the destruction around him.)

JONATHAN (CONT'D): What ... happened?

MEL: It doesn't matter.

JONATHAN: Mel --

MEL: You forget something?

JONATHAN: You. You're coming with me.

MEL: No, I'm not.

JONATHAN: You said you'd do anything.

MEL: I said a lot of things.

JONATHAN: So you were lying.

MEL: You're the one who's a liar.

JONATHAN: This thing. It killed your parents, it killed my parents -- if I'm not careful, it'll kill me, too.

MEL: Why is it up to me, then?

JONATHAN: Because there's no one else.

MEL: You shouldn't have come back --

JONATHAN: I had to!

MEL: Why, for this?

(She takes a tool from her pack and slices into her palm, deliberately, and holds the wound out to him.)

MEL (CONT'D): Is this what you came for?

JONATHAN: Jesus!

MEL: Isn't this what you need?

JONATHAN: Please. Mel.

(He reaches into his pocket for a bandana. He takes her hand, and gently tends to her wound. She regards this, flat affect, detached.)

MEL: When I came here, I felt lucky. It was safe. But that's not enough. I've never done anything that wasn't -

- that wasn't by chance, that was something by my choice. To be lucky? That's just letting life happen to you without putting up a fight. I'm not going to do that anymore.

JONATHAN: What are you going to do?

MEL: I'm leaving. I need to see if I can survive. On my own.

JONATHAN: But nobody does.

(He has finished wrapping her hand.)

JONATHAN (CONT'D): On their own? Nobody does.

(MEL's detachment crumbles, and she begins to weep.)

(Then, DEBORAH enters, clutching a bundle in the crook of one arm, and holding the knife with her opposite hand. DEBORAH has blood on her clothing, her hands, her face.)

DEBORAH: Sh... Sh... It's quiet now. It's OK. It's OK. It's over. (*To the bundle in the crook of her arm.*) You don't need to worry: it's over.

(DEBORAH takes in a big breath and sighs.)

DEBORAH (CONT'D): Listen to that! It's so quiet!

MEL: What happened?

DEBORAH: (*To Mel.*) It's over. It's finally over.

MEL: Are you hurt?

DEBORAH: It turns out you don't need to be strong -- you just need to be quick.

(DEBORAH smiles, looking down at the baby.)

MEL: Is that...?

DEBORAH: Yes. A beautiful boy.

MEL: And Sarah?

DEBORAH: You'd be proud of me: I cut the cord.

(DEBORAH hands MEL the knife. It is slick with blood, and she lets it fall.)

DEBORAH (CONT'D): You didn't think I could do it, did you. I don't think I believed it either. But I did. Quick and deep. And then it was over. (*Beat*.) There was so much blood.

MEL: Where's Sarah?

DEBORAH: Where she fell.

(MEL runs off, and JONATHAN approaches DEBORAH.)

JONATHAN: Can I... let me see him.

DEBORAH: It's all right.

JONATHAN: Let me see the baby, Deborah.

DEBORAH: He was born like this. Blue. Like an angel.

(DEBORAH hands the baby to JONATHAN, who quickly checks for any vital signs.)

DEBORAH (CONT'D): See? Isn't he perfect? Sarah would have loved him, too. (*Beat.*) There was more blood than I expected.

JONATHAN: Is Sarah...?

DEBORAH: Gone. I couldn't stop him --

(MEL returns, and a quick look to JONATHAN confirms DEBORAH's account. During the following, JONATHAN listens for the baby's heartbeat.)

DEBORAH (CONT'D): I mean, I stopped him, but too late. (*Beat.*) Zed came running -- I had just taken the baby, and turned to see him, running. I think he knew, the moment he saw him. Maybe I could have stopped him -- I wasn't thinking! He pushed past me, and he was on top of her, her neck in his hands -- and I... stopped him. It was so easy! A quick cut and -- over. (*Beat.*) There was so much blood.

(Brief pause.)

DEBORAH (CONT'D): I loved him.

MEL: I know.

(Quickly, gently, JONATHAN swaddles the body of the baby. It's clear, in the following, that Deborah is neither insane, nor incapable.)

DEBORAH: But if he killed Sarah, where would he stop? I had to protect the rest of us. I had to protect my baby. (*Beat.*) You don't think she knew, do you? No. She didn't. I'm glad for that, at least. (*Beat.*) I can't bury them myself. (*To Mel.*) Should I burn them? I'll burn them.

(DEBORAH holds her arms out for the baby, and JONA-THAN hands it to her.)

DEBORAH (CONT'D): *(To the baby.)* I'll find a better resting spot for you. *(Beat.)* They'll take good care of you, Mel.

MEL: What?

DEBORAH: Where you're going. They'll take good care of you.

MEL: Deborah, I'll stay.

DEBORAH: I have the girls. We'll be fine.

MEL: I'll stay -- I'll help.

DEBORAH: No. They're expecting you. And this is mine now. What I deserve. *(Beat.)* It's not such a terrible thing to be afraid.

(DEBORAH kisses MEL on the cheek.)

DEBORAH (CONT'D): It's not such a terrible thing.

(DEBORAH exits.)

(JONATHAN and MEL remain. MEL picks up the knife, and cleans the blood from it, sheaths it.)

MEL: She's right. I pretend that I'm not afraid. But I am. Afraid of being alone, afraid of staying here, afraid of the world. I was thinking about our parents. Your parents sent you away... to survive, don't you think? And mine would have, I'm sure. But I don't think they would have wanted me to hide... which is all I've done. But... I thought if I could learn to survive, with all that fear -- If I could prove to myself that I could do it, by myself... But if I only live for myself, then I only die for myself. And then I might as well give up.

(She sees JONATHAN's book, and holds it out to him.)

MEL (CONT'D): Here. You'll need this.

JONATHAN: It's yours.

MEL: But --

JONATHAN: I want you to keep it.

(She nods, holding the book to her chest.)

MEL: Would I be there for long?

JONATHAN: I don't know.

MEL: I'd miss them... Deborah, the girls.

JONATHAN: We could check on them.

MEL: We could. (*Beat.*) Though... maybe they'd be better off without us.

JONATHAN: Maybe they would.

MEL: You wouldn't leave me there -- forever.

JONATHAN: No.

(A pause. A decision.)

MEL: OK.

JONATHAN: You'll go?

MEL: Yes. But first -- I want to see them.

JONATHAN: What?

MEL: The bees. If you've really found them. Take me to them -- Just let me see them. And then... I'll go anywhere you want.

(JONATHAN thinks about this for a moment.)

JONATHAN: OK.

MEL: Really?

JONATHAN: Yes. *(Beat.)* For you.

(She turns, climbs the tree, and picks the apple, which she hands to him.)

MEL: Here: Trade for the book. Plant the seeds.

JONATHAN: Mel, you know that won't work.

MEL: I know... The seeds won't grow into this kind of apple. But it will grow into something, won't it? Maybe something better.

(She cuts the apple in half to reveal the small, black seeds.)

MEL (CONT'D): We should pick apples from every tree, and plant every seed. You could take hundreds of seeds back with you, plant hundreds of trees --

JONATHAN: And have hundreds of failures?

MEL: It's only a failure if you only want one kind of answer. (Holding up a seed.) Look at that: there's a secret in here. Aren't you curious about that? What we know and what we have... it's not enough. But here: here's something we can't even imagine.

(She hands half of the apple to JONATHAN.)

MEL (CONT'D): I don't know how to be ready for this.

JONATHAN: It'll be OK, Mel.

MEL: No. Not Mel. I'm not that person anymore. Call me Melissa. (*Beat.*) That's who I have to be.

JONATHAN: Well. Melissa. Hello. (*Beat.*) Ready?

MEL: Yes.

JONATHAN: It's not the world you knew, out there.

MEL: I know. But I don't want it to be.

(She takes a bite, then he does as well.)

END OF PLAY.

NOTES

NOTES

NOTES